PLAY IT!

THE LITTLE BOOK OF SONG TITLES

CREATED & DESIGNED BY
TEECEE DESIGN STUDIO

Thank you so much for your purchase.

I really do hope that this book has helped you,
even in some small way.

Would you like to see different designs/styles?

I am always very happy to hear from customers,
so please feel free to email me on

teeceedesignstudio@yahoo.com

9 781675 072912